PARENTS
LOVE

DARRELL SOMERS

PARENTS LOVE

© 2023 DARRELL SOMERS

Adriel Publishing

Printed in the U.S.A.

Cover artwork by Darrell Somers

Cover design by Darrell Somers & Elizabeth Lawless

ISBN: 979-8-9896554-2-7

This book is dedicated to
my Parents who have
always given me
inspiration and love.
I miss and love both of you,
there is not a day that something
does not remind me of
both of you.

TABLE OF CONTENTS

Actions

It is hard to make a decision on the behalf of someone else's thoughts.

There will be some that will think it's all a plot.

The darkness is so bright that my eyes can't adjust.

Not everyone will understand my reasons for my actions of trust.

It is okay if others condemn and move out of my life.

For the people that walk out of my life, know this will cause me strife.

I know that all my actions will not be accepted by others.

I will always love you just like a sister or brother.

My wish is that no one is ever put in this room of severity.

Where some think my actions is to bring myself prosperity.

For the people who do not understand, it is not my job to help with your confusion.

My actions are not mine; it's to bring another one's life conclusion.

BLACK HOLE

I feel like I am living my life in a black hole space.

Not knowing up from down it's so dark I can't even see my face.

There are times when the darkness can make me feel safe and secure.

At times I have one of those days that even in the dark everything is crystal clear and easy to endure.

Climbing out of the blackness seems like an invincible task.

I think the only way out is to put on a perfection mask.

The black hole of gloom is always controlling my existence.

The nothingness always has a way of breaking down my resistance.

I am now sitting in my blackness with Van Gogh thoughts running through my mind.

Wondering why have all the people in my life gone and left me behind.

I am trying to catch all the light beams that penetrate the dark and touches my soul.

With each beam I capture gives me hope that I
have paid my toll.

With a little luck tomorrow will bring more light
to guide my path out of the black hole of darkness.

CALM

I look into your soul's light.

It shows the pain in your life.

The world can be hard and relentless.

Your mind's self-worth is merciless.

I wish I could lift the burdens from your mind.

So, you don't have to feel withdrawn and hard to find.

The power of the world's veil makes it seem colder.

Carrying these burdens on your shoulders.

Don't let the pain put out your light.

Rip the veils in your mind to let in the radiating light.

Never walk close to the edge alone.

Never worry about the cast of the first stone.

CHANGE

The world outside is changing it's hard to find things I recognize.

Understand I am not trying to stop the revise.

There is no bad feeling about the changing times.

I am not saying that years gone by were the best of times.

Enjoy every day because tomorrow will be different from today.

But always remember people and places that remind you of happier days.

Keep the happy times from past and future in the canyons in your mind.

CRAZY

There is a piece of my thoughts I put on paper.

My mind has too many thoughts battling that feel like a vapor.

Memories can be like a movie in my head that plays on repeat.

Words seem to flow on the paper like drugs on a back street.

The thoughts in my mind that I write down can seem strange.

Often as I am writing them down it feels I am deranged.

When the movie plays the only way to hit pause is to write.

What I write doesn't always make since, I am trying to stop the fight.

Writing feels like rain washing away the minds thoughts that are hazy.

It is the only way to stay sane and not go CRAZY.

Dark

There are times I feel like a lost soul.

Wandering through life out in the cold.

Everywhere I turn there is darkness.

From the darkness a hand reaches out with brightness.

I touch it and the darkness is gone.

My world is lit with hope and promise.

No more being a doubting Thomas.

Like every other time it is hard staying in this moment.

It is hard fighting the dark opponent.

The dark will put questions and doubt in my head.

That brings darkness and dread.

Like always the Savior True reaches out his hand.

DECISION

I walk alone into a less full house.

I walk without four paws following.

I will miss the corky personality.

Just like all the ones before.

I will miss the familiar welcome.

The unique warm greeting.

Every one of them was different.

It is hard to make life altering decisions.

Trying to understand what is best.

Putting your own selfish desires aside.

The burden is heavy.

But the suffering is much heavier.

Every life is hard to lose.

If there were that magic pill.

I would of gave all for it.

Rest for now, without any pain.

Until we meet again.

DOUBLE FEATURE CREATURE

I lay down to sleep.

Sleep doesn't come by counting sheep.

My mind is always overloaded.

How could I have handled that?

What should I have said there?

My mind feels eroded.

Never giving me a minute's rest.

Always questioning like it is a test.

Wondering if I am the only one?

That deals with this mind creature.

Wishing that I could hide or outrun.

Knowing it is always a double feature.

I hope to get at least an hour of peaceful sleep.

DREAM

I am always amazed at beautiful days.

How calm my soul feels listening to nature's praise.

I relax under the tree of dreams.

Drifting down a calm stream.

Suddenly I see the face of the one who made me.

My world is filled with colors I have never seen.

The music I hear is sung by a choir in perfect harmony.

I see the cup that was made with perfect carpentry.

All the questions have been taken away.

I fell to my knees with my family to pray.

The bird's song opens my eyes.

To the beautiful blue colors in the skies.

DREAMING TREE

In the shade I will lie.

With a smile on my face.

Resting under the dreaming tree.

Resting my eyes in this space.

My mind is carefree.

Dreaming of things in my past.

Good times with family and friends.

But also, the bad, how they contrast.

The bad it is like a zoom lens.

I wonder how I can be forgiven.

Will I be let into heaven.

I open my eyes and know how to make it right.

I stand and step back into the light.

DREAMING

There are storm clouds forming over the social flower.

The clout will release the kraken with all its power.

I can't wrap my mind around the way people think they are better by the color of their skin.

What happened to the days where opinions could be respected and not be condemned for a win?

Why can't we listen to others without using bully tactics with name calling and threats of violence?

Don't make hasty judgments because you're probably wrong so just keep silence.

Looking at the city through a looking glass you can see multi colors in the sky.

People dream about a happy place where everyone has the best piece of the pie.

The music in my ear sends me to an imaginary place of marshmallow billow fragments.

I can see people loving and embracing each other just for being there with no bias or judgments.

The sounds get louder with dancing like no one is watching smiling faces.

The world is celebrating the beat of life with happiness and equal mined cases.

Happy Happy Joy Joy with Mother Nature's shine.

EXPECTATIONS

It's a burden that they will use to push down on you.

They will never see the pain that it has caused you.

Blood should never cause so much pain.

You are feeling sadness because others have betrayed your trust.

Nothing cuts deeper than the blade of trust.

Wondering where all your family and friends have gone.

When you were young it seemed everyone was on your side.

Then life shows not all were really standing by your side.

As an adult you see how greed can win beliefs.

Others will wear the mask of false faith so they can hide from you.

It's hard to love someone that doesn't love you.

When you draw your last breath, know that you will be surrounded by love.

All the time that is wasted on hate will be washed away.

All doubts will be in the past, all the agony will be eroded away.

Expectations that others have put on you are always too high to reach.

This way they can feel good about their own expectations they will never reach.

FALL

Halloween thrills with the excitement of treats that are abound.

Christmas time gifts are on the minds of kids all around.

Cold weather has peak the imaginations of adults snuggling by the fire.

This brings on the anticipation of the bearded wonder with his entire flying deer sire.

Before the holy jolly man appears the boogie man comes first to raise the adrenalin.

Putting more logs on the fire to have shadows on the walls for scary lighting.

The fall leaves in full color can calm the most pessimistic hearts.

Going to a pumpkin patch see all different colored pumpkins on all the carts.

Fall is one of the most wonderful times of the year.

I will be having a party for the Holidays with friends and family serving pumpkin beer.

We must never forget the day we share a wild beast feast.

Rush rush rush non-stop the holiday season is here spending money will not cease.

Then the cold weather sets in cloths are tight from the holiday cheer.

With that thought I think I will have another pumpkin beer.

FAULT

I am so lonely.

You don't come around here anymore.

I find myself struggling through the day.

With not much to say.

All I do is sit around thinking.

But there is nothing helping.

Trying to not start drinking.

I understand I was to blame.

That is why you don't care anymore.

It's my fault, I put out the flame.

Your words cut like a knife.

It may take all my life.

But look at my face.

Listen to my voice.

I am trying to find a place.

To repair my choice.

So, we can be friends.

Once again.

FOLLOW

The first day I truly heard you speak to me.

I knew my soul was free.

You made my heart sing.

You became my everything.

I believe in my destiny.

That you set before me.

There are days harder than others to follow my path.

When the world unleashes its wrath.

There are more days my thoughts are crystal clear.

I understand why I am here with no fear.

Everyone has their convictions.

That something that they have a connection.

My connection was a Jew.

My Savior True.

FOLLOWING

It's like going to a party and not knowing anyone.

And yet you're the host!

It's like trying to live your life as Jesus would.

And always condemning while you boast!

It's like thinking you're walking in the light.

And your actions are dark!

It's like going to a concert.

And you're the only one in the park!

It's like trying to tell someone about your faith.

And you want to touch the wounds for proof!

It's like professing your faith.

And they say now let's hear the truth!

FORGIVENESS

You come at me like a leach wanting to suck out
my existence.

Behind your eyes there is nothing but black and
distance.

My heart is being pulled out of my chest with
blood red sadness.

All you think about is stealing the bright shinny
gold that was given.

I have given all that I should, but it seems there is a
never ending miss trust.

We will never be happy without forgiveness, always
using words to thrust.

Just know through all the hatefulness of words I am
here.

I am dreaming for the time we might be family
once again to wipe the tears.

HEADED HOME

When I don't need this body anymore.

My soul will take flight and soar.

Know that my last embrace with you meant so much.

I will always remember that touch.

Please don't let your thoughts roam.

Because I am headed home.

When you hear sounds that remind you of me.

Know that I am by your side and will never leave.

There will come a time when we embrace again.

There will no longer be any pain.

I will be waiting on that day.

When the Savior True will say.

Welcome home my faithful believer.

HOME

If your light was put out today.

Where would you go?

Would you fly through the sky of blue.

Would you fall to your knees.

Would you lower your head from His glow.

Could you speak for all that is due.

In the presence of the Savior True.

Would you embrace.

All the ones that have gone before.

Smile as you see their beautiful face.

Know that you are home.

No more pain, only Love.

When you see the Trinity sitting on their Throne.

I Am

All that I am.

All that I will be.

Can be heard in the songs.

They sing in the Church.

Jesus came, and Jesus died.

His face can be seen throughout the day.

My Faith is the thing that keeps me going.

You are my rhythm, melody, and my rock.

Until the day you take me home.

If I Die Tomorrow

If I die tomorrow.

Know that I Loved you all.

And that I am going home.

I will miss you.

Until the day we will embrace once again.

I made many mistakes.

But loving all of you was never a mistake.

IF YOU DON'T LIKE ME

If you disagree with me brother that's OK!!!

It doesn't affect me in anyway.

Always letting gossip from loose lips changes your opinion.

Listening to false dialog can be a dangerous position.

I don't worry about what you say.

I won't let it ruin my perfect day.

Living my life without pressure of what others think I should be.

Just because I don't think the way you think doesn't mean I have to flee.

Too much of the world today is you're wrong if you don't think the same as me.

Talking about others to make you feel better is not the key.

Brother just let me be!!

INSANITY

The world outside can make you feel insane.

Making you stumble and fall.

Is it better to feel pain?

Or feel nothing at all?

Always looking for that soul saving resolution.

Never giving to the Savior True.

He is your soul saving resolution.

Just give yourself and stop being blue.

He Reigns.

Glory to God he Reigns.

Because he Reigns, his blood makes us whole.

Because he Reigns, we have eternal life.

Glory to God He Reigns.

His power can open your soul.

With free will choose the Savior True.

Even if he is denied.

Like Peter did three times.

He will be there with open arms.

Let his blood wash over you.

To open the pearly gates.

To give you strength to face each day.

He Reigns.

Glory to God he Reigns.

Because he Reigns, we have eternal life.

Because he Reigns, his blood makes us whole.

Glory to God he Reigns.

Leave all your fears behind.

See how high you can fly.

Wasted time trying to find.

When all you needed is to take his hand.

When it is your time.

You will know you are complete.

Walking to light as I climb.

Being greeted with a hug as he sits in his seat the Savior True.

Telling you welcome home.

My faithful believer.

He Reigns.

Glory to God he Reigns.

Because he Reigns, we have eternal life.

Because he Reigns, his blood makes us whole.

Glory to God he Reigns.

As we live our life's.

Under the power of the King of King's.

The power of his blood washes all strives.

Listen to the Angle's sing.

Didn't know I was blind.

Until I saw the Savior True.

Now all my thoughts are kind.

As laugh and smile standing with the Savior True.

He Reigns.

Glory to God he Reigns.

Because he Reigns, we have eternal life.

Because he Reigns, his blood makes us whole.

Glory to God he Reigns.

I give all my soul.

To my Savior True.

This life will always take a toll.

As my heart and soul flew.

All I want is everyone to take this trip.

There is no packing necessary.

There is no planning required.

All that is asked is faith.

Faith in something you can't touch.

Faith in something that some say is foolish.

Faith to give all to.

Faith to know you will fail.

Faith to know you are saved in the blood of the Savior True.

Stop being a doubting Thomas.

Being of little Faith.

INSIDE

Judging someone by the way they look.

Your special if you can by the cover of the book.

Thinking you know.

Turns out not to be so.

No one know what's deep inside.

It would help if everyone had a guide.

It would be nice if we could feel their heartbeat.

Being able to tell from a heartbeat, what a sweet treat.

You might know someone well.

But not always can tell.

Knowing what is inside there are only two.

The person and the Savior True.

JAMES 1:5-6

When you're weak.

You can always bend at the knees.

To draw strength from the One that Cures.

Being a believer doesn't mean you're perfect.

A true believer knows they are a sinner.

When you commit the same sin over and over.

You feel so useless.

Hallelujah, Hallelujah He Reigns

The One that was sent for you and me.

He Reigns with mercy.

Jesus loves you.

Jesus doesn't question your faults.

He will always keep trying to make you Holy.

There is always good news.

Listen to Savior True news for you.

The True One always loves you.

You are perfection.

Being a sinner.

Because you were made by the Deliverer.

The seed was planted.

He is the cultivator.

The Savior's blood can work miracles.

If only you will let it.

I know that you are near.

And I feel that you are here.

But I never felt the call.

I have never seen the signs others have claimed they saw.

Is my faith not strong enough.

Or is it my sin that keeps me from seeing.

Wondering why others have seen your signs.

I have not seen, am I not part of the plans.

I'm not asking to see the burning bush.

I have faith not because I have seen.

But because I believe.

I do wonder why I have so many questions.

Does this mean that I am not as close to you.

As I feel my faith is.

JUNE 11, 1983

I can't believe the day we fell in love.

It seems like yesterday.

How time flies when your life is perfection.

I never thought I would find True Love.

There you were standing in my way.

My heart opened in your direction.

It has been 40 years since I said I do.

Two young kids holding a dream.

With not much more than Love.

There were days when my mind was blue.

I'm sure there were times you wanted to scream.

There were more days filled with Love.

Out of the forty years we have had so many good ones.

I'm so glad you get my sense of humor.

Living with me can't be easy.

I hope you have had more days filled with fun.
Anyway, that is the rumor.

I need your Love; I know coming from me it
sounds cheesy.

KNOWLEDGE

Stop listening to fools.

That always break the rules.

Fools only care about what's in it for me.

Sometimes that is hard to see.

If you have listened don't cry.

Just open your mind and learn why.

Set yourself free.

With knowledge from the learning tree.

A fool's advice will never come free.

LAST DAY

If you knew it was your last day,

Who would you want to see, and what would you say?

I think if I knew, I would want to see or at least talk with all friends and family.

I would tell them how much I love them and don't feel sad about my calamity.

My wish is that they remember the times of laugher and friendship.

Don't waste time with any hard feelings they may have had during our script.

I want them to know that I have nothing but love for them in my heart.

That I will be waiting with open arms during our time apart.

Never feel sad that I am not able to be with them.

Know that when they think of me, I am spiritually with them.

So please when I go to the great unknown clearsighted.

Celebrate with happiness and joy knowing one day we will be reunited.

LESSON

My eye grew heavy.

As I laid back and started dreaming.

I was transformed to a beautiful place.

I arose and started exploring my surroundings.

I asked everyone I met where am I.

They just smiled and waved.

I asked who was in charge.

A voice answered we are all here because of our aggressions.

I noticed the beauty of this place started fading.

How do we return to the place where we started.

They all fell to their knees.

Started praying.

I fell to my knees.

My eyes opened and I was home.

Life Is Too Short

We are assured not one second longer than we are due.

Life seems so slow while we are young and carefree.

But as we get older, we ask where the time went.

Life is too short to be thinking of the future or the past.

There is a reason for the path that are cast.

Live for the right now and not what has happened or will happen.

In the end know that you have lived life and loved to the fullest with no regrets.

LIFE STRUGGLES

Drifting further away.
From the one who calls my name.
Never answering the call.
I'm the only one to blame.

How oh how will I?
Make my way back.
To where I belong.
To the one that calls me home.

There are days when I feel.
The same as when you first called my name.
Then there are days I search for redemption.
Searching in all the wrong directions.

The memory of you is like a still frame in my mind.
They seem to fade in time.
If only I could hit rewind.
Dreams are like a projector.
My mind is the director.

How oh how will I?
Make my way back.
To where I belong.
To the one that calls me home.

Why do I act Like doubting Thomas?
Always asking why me?
My Savior True.
What is it that you see?

You are my Lord and Savior.
So why do I still wander with bad behavior.
The hardest thing is to seek perfection.
With my sinful affliction.

How oh how will I?
Make my way back.
To where I belong.
To the one that calls me home.

LIFETIME

As my story is told of how I lived my life.

There will be talk of strife.

There are many ways to look at one's life during a life time.

Love and hate can walk hand in hand in crime.

In life your actions can never satisfy everyone.

I will admit that there were things I would have liked to have undone.

If I offended someone maybe they didn't truly known me.

Knowledge in understanding me is the key.

Some may say I was wound tight.

While other will say he was a bit of a blithe.

Both are probably true.

How much you knew and treated me would be the clue.

You can't please everyone so you might as well please yourself.

LISTEN

I often wonder where I would be without laughter and love.

Love is the word that speaks to everyone on the wings of a dove.

People will continuously act in a way that makes others fester.

They always come up with ways to try and make others feel like a jester.

Just image what would happen if the world would start caring about all creation.

I wish we could shine a light on the world that opens minds to a moral revolution.

People will always run from their fears of other opinions with fierceness.

If we would just listen and reflect on what others say with thoughtfulness.

The world today is consumed with selfishness so we do not listen to others articulate.

Just because you feel wronged doesn't mean your side is accurate.

Our time on this plant is short so why spend your time with hate.

Open up your thought to a world full of Love and a positive fate.

LONG ROAD

The long road of life can shine like gold; the glare can be an illusion.

If you see thru the glare it is all a grand perception.

Some hide imperfections by looking through rose colored glasses.

It is not always a life of perfection, like most of the masses.

I am just a fool trying to navigate through this thing called life.

The perception is that I have it all under control without strife.

If you could see the inside, the chaos that is my existence.

Turmoil can blind all that is good in life crushing your resistance.

The true people in your life know that you are not perfect and bold.

It is better to have friends that are golden than a paved road of gold.

Peace is knowing friends and family will always be there with you.

Through this long road of Mayhem called life.

Loss

The short time we had together.

I will cherish it for the rest of my life.

You were so strong with your fight.

I don't understand why you had to endure such pain and suffering.

My wish is that I could've stopped the suffering.

I would have taken all your pain and suffering, but my hands were tied.

Know that I felt your pain and suffering every time you cried.

The only thing that consoles me in losing you is no more pain.

That one thought keeps me sane.

One day I will be able embrace you with the Savior True.

Until that day I will never stop speaking to you.

Looking for your signs in the world around me.

Knowing you are always with me.

LOST TIME

If there is someone you care about.

You had a big blow out.

Now is the time to mend that relationship.

There are no guarantees for a round trip.

Once they are gone.

All you will have is their song.

Time is not yours to keep.

So don't sleep.

Memories are like photos in your mind.

They can fade in time.

Dreams are like a projector.

Your mind is the director.

Looking for redemption.

Always in the wrong direction.

LUCK

Every time I reach for the brass ring; it slips right through my finger.

I buy a ticket for the train and don't get to ride because I linger.

My lottery ticket is a winner, before I can cash it in it gets lost.

I go to a restaurant when the ticket comes, I can't afford the cost.

I find the perfect job, but it seems I'm too qualified or too old.

The home I wanted has asbestoses and black mold.

I find a great sale; it was over yesterday.

I have big plans outside this weekend, and it rains that day.

Even with all my bad luck that seems to follow me.

I am the luckiest person to have family & friends that Love me.

Love is the greatest thing you can own.

MERCY

How close is Mercy?

How long to feel His touch?

Does it take time for my controversy?

Are my demons too much?

The Redeemer's hand is always there.

To catch you when you fall.

The Savior True will always care.

All you need to do is call.

Hope is eternal.

If you believe in His words.

Always looking Supernal.

Speaking so your voice goes as high as the birds.

How close are you?

How far am I?

MIND GAMES

Everything will be ok just trust your doing your best.

Don't worry about what the bitter hearts are going to say.

They will always try to bully and put you to the test.

Haters will never stop hating while you seem ok.

You're an emotional person so keep strong.

Everyone has the same fragile weakness.

Worried about what others think will keep you playing their games.

Trust your mind and live life to its fullness.

Always use your common sense and never reach into the flames.

When bullies don't have the upper hand, they will shrink.

The choices you make should never make you tense.

Keep your mind straight never meander to the brink.

You are special and you are the only one you need to impress.

MOM

I am here mom standing alone without you trying to figure out which way to turn.

I think about you every moment that I am awake; being here makes my stomach churn.

I think back about all the good and bad times we went through it makes me sad.

I wonder how you ever made it day to day without losing it and being filled with fad.

I understand that you were tired and wanted to be with loved ones always being in loneliness.

I want to thank you for teaching me how to face hardships with strength and boldness.

I have days all I think about is how I can go on without you, but I know you would not want that.

I have problems getting out of bed at times but I wonder how you didn't fall to the mat.

I will try my best to be the person you wanted me to become to live life to the fullest.

Having you in my life and being my mom was the coolest.

MOONLIGHT

You brighten my world like a shooting star in moonlight.

The glow from your moonbeams gives me hope that is so bright.

You shine like a bright star in the darkest sky.

You smell just like Christmas chia.

Know that I'm yours through time and space.

Open up your heart so I see my place.

You are so beautiful just the sight of you makes me melt.

Dancing by moonlight is the best feeling I have ever felt.

You make me smile even if it's only your lovely smell.

The words for me don't come easy if you can't tell.

My world would shatter if you were not in my life.

It's a beautiful day when I wake and you're my wife.

The passion you have for the ones you love.

Fits me like a warm glove.

You will never be alone.

Because know that you are home.

My Guitar

I jumped a ride on the crazy train.

The engine is rumbling down the track.

Keeping with the sway of the train.

I play my guitar to the beat of the rails clack.

Not remembering where I just left.

Or where I am from.

Knowing all I have comes from theft.

Still my guitar I strum.

I feel the strain.

With the rocking of the train.

Always remembering what people say.

That I am lazy because I don't pay.

I feel this life was made for me.

Playing my guitar and being free.

OPEN

Surrender your heart and soul with no judgment.

The nostalgic fear with opening your emotions can be full of pain.

Climb aboard the passion train with no anxiety of how long you can ride.

Get that ticket punched and never look back thinking this is insane.

Don't go through life with blinders.

Not everyone is trying to take advantage of your loving environment.

Yes there will be some riders that will see you as a stain.

But never let them take your love or pride.

Swallow that bittersweet pill and keep riding the train.

The world is always better when we are kinder.

It is always good to live life with confidence without being arrogant.

Somedays there will be sunshine and some will be rain.

But never stop riding the train and keep the sunlight and wind in your face.

PARENTS LOVE

Under the dreaming tree.

My parents came to me.

I am sorry that we are not there.

Don't think we do not care.

Know that when you speak to us, we listen to you.

When you need a hug, we embrace you.

When you walk with, or you're being carried by the Savior True.

We are walking behind both of you.

Just know that just because we have been called home.

Our Love has not been put on hold.

I am glad I was made from their mold.

PERFECTION

From across the room, I see your perfection.

Your persona emits a high volume of seduction.

The thought of you even looking at a guy like me is implausible.

I watch from across the room with your long legs and high heels that are unimaginable.

You are walking right at me, and I feel my heartbeat throughout my whole body.

The smile that you smile makes me feel that I have just drunk a hot toddy.

You touch my hand a tingle goes up my spine like shock waves through my soul.

It's hard to keep my mind and thoughts under control.

Tell me why your touch always makes me feel weak in the knees.

I feel I am in a 57 speedster, and I have the keys.

Your love gives my body the air I need to survive another breath.

PRIDE

There are days I feel like a Saint.

Is that pride talking in my head.

Does my light brighten the dark.

I need to have self-restraint.

Keep my thoughts on the one that bled.

My thoughts spin like a ride at the amusement park.

All days I know I am a Sinner.

No matter how hard I pound my chest.

Sin is my prison.

Even if I feel like a winner.

I am a sinner that is blessed.

Because he has Risen.

PROBLEM

It seems problems chase me daily.

Sometimes they overwhelm me.

So, I turn to a bottle.

Trying to drink a lake full.

Only to find out they have a raft.

Does my problem make me stronger?

Or make me smarter?

Will it teach me not to do the same thing?

If it is true History always repeats.

How can I avoid the problem?

If I destroy what cause the problem.

Will that mean it will not happen again?

Or does that mean I will forget and then repeat it?

REAL WORLD

You're the sugar in my drink.

My mind is racing so fast it's hard to think.

Just the thought of you sends me into a dream
state.

I am flying higher than a UFO flying plate.

I am cruising faster than the speed of light.

I am trying to catch a glimpse of your beauty that
shines bright.

While in my dream I see all the beauty of this
dream world.

But I am an idiot trying to find something as
beautiful as my real world.

I come out my dream with a smile knowing that
you will be by my side.

And my mind is filled with Jubilation and pride.

REFLECTION

In the blink of an eye, we are flying through a canyon.

To the left of me is a buffalo with wings flying faster than a yelling minion.

To the right of me you are in a tie-dye-colored TUTU bomb diving into the aquatic.

The water is changing colors with every dive and the ripples of the waves make you iconic.

We soar higher than the mountains where the eagles fly above the marshmallow cloud.

Ascending through the turmoil of life with the winds of change abound.

Flying above the fall-colored trees in the year that the world must change normal life.

Most can fly with the change of the day; others look at change with strife.

Looking in the mirrors of the sky and not appreciating what is concealed.

Hoping Picasso, like the people below, can soar to the heights that are revealed.

The colors of the rainbow blend together knowing they all belong to the same rainbow.

Pigs fly to meet the struggles of the day with the flying cow.

As we soar through this wormhole of life hoping for the light, we will be able to find.

Recalling the good old days were not bright advancement of respect to humankind.

Each whisper of the wind gives more knowledge to not repeat the last.

Struggling with familiarity of life and trying not to do the same recurrences of the past.

Knowing that we are all part of the human race we need to soar together.

Let our differences bring us together with respect and reverence.

RIDE

Riding on the last train to nowhere.

The train stops at the end of the line.

The eyes are looking to see my next move.

Feeling frozen from their stare.

Looking around for a sign.

The air is so thick of how they disapprove.

Do I throw up my hands and quit.

Or do I stand and keep moving forward.

Not giving in to the shadows.

Step back into the light slit.

If only things where straight forward.

The lows might not be so low.

My daily ride on the train in the caverns in my mind.

SEEK

I close my eyes and find myself searching for something.

Not sure what my search will bring.

I sit beside a river flowing with majestic purple calmness.

Why do I feel the need to condemn others for my loneliness?

I walk into the water letting my thoughts wash over me.

The water rushes through my mind so I can clearly see.

What I seek is just being loved.

SHINE

Silence from the Dead eyes behind the face that seems to never cry.

One look makes me want to die.

Why does it make me feel this way?

Your total disregard at times makes me fray.

I wished I could see what goes on in your head.

Your blank eyes can make me fall to my knees and feel misled.

I wished you could feel my mood?

I try not to say things that can seem rude.

It seems I'm always looking through the ring of fire.

My knight's armor is shiny and ready to be a squire.

Let the shine put light behind your dead eyes.

Breathe and try to keep your brain calm from its hellfire.

Don't expect much from me chasing things around in your minds troubles.

I wonder if it will be a difficult day with your mind's struggles.

Let your mind relax in the shinning light.

STRENGTH

The world today is so unclear.

Who is right or who is wrong?

Standing for beliefs can bring fear.

Trying to make the right decision and stay strong.

Searching for strength somebody stole.

Stole straight out of my soul.

STUPID

The world around me makes me feel clumsy and stupid.

There are times I feel that I can make sense of my domain.

I am reminded how unwise my thoughts can be by the reactions of my cupid.

My mind has too many voices talking at once, trying to stay sane.

The voices argue about how I should feel about Rupert.

I am so happy when the voices in my head ride in a plane.

I get tired doing this sleep walk dance, when I am the culprit.

Thinking I can cope with all the negativity spewing trying to keep me in pain.

It's not sane to listen to the voices telling me how I am stupid.

Always using the crutch that it's not me and I am not vain.

SUNLIGHT

The morning sunlight falls on her face.

She looks so happy and content sleeping.

I whisper in her ear how beautiful she is with grace.

Her eyes open slowly with a sexy smile that is leaping.

We lie in bed passing the morning enjoying life, while we embrace.

There is no place else I would rather be than with her dreaming.

Laying there not saying anything, my eyes closed using my hands to trace.

My soul is happy and content lying there just being.

Hours have pasted, it feels like only moments staring into deep space.

I wish time would stop for a while, so I can hold on to this feeling.

Morning has turned into night; still, we are in bed fighting the pillow race.

We wake to the realty of the worlds demands, with only memory's staring at the ceiling.

Waiting for the day I can see the sunlight again on her beautiful face.

THE DIRTY SOUL OF THE CITY

The dirty soul of the city.

Doesn't show pity.

You need to have a strong will.

Or you will be paying the bill.

The streets will leave you wondering.

Do you have the will to take another breath?

The darkness will squeeze the last strength out of your soul.

The dirty soul of the city.

Will take your soul if you let it.

After midnight the city comes alive.

All dirty souls thrive.

In the darkness of the streets.

Guard your soul to keep.

Emerge from the darkness to the light.

Whispering in the dark will not keep the darkness at bay.

You need to let your actions be your guide from the darkness.

Let light shine through your soul.

So, the lost souls of the dirty city can capture the light that shines in you.

The world outside can make you feel insane.

THE END

My dream is that our love for each other doesn't stop.

By politics or who is our elected leader.

Is your love real if you stop caring because of a leader?

With each person who is in charge what has really changed?

My heart would hurt if you stopped singing our song.

I need your help to sing my chorus.

How do you replace a voice that will not sing with you?

Is the silence in your heart worth the animosity?

When your voice is gone and leaves your nothingness.

You will have no use for bitterness?

I regret that we can't respect instead of hate.

If we disagree who is right and who is wrong.

How can you condemn if you feel condemned.

Every living thing has the same rights as you.

If you hate, does it affect you or them?

At the end will it truly matter?

THE PATH

I walk on this path that has been put in front of me taking one step at a time.

Sometimes this path is uphill and muddy and still I take one step at a time.

All I want is a path that has meaning and gives me hope.

Hope to be at peace while walking down each slope.

I have a never ending quest to reach the next mountain peak.

Appreciating the adventure that my path has set before me while learning to stay meek.

I remain mentally positive while on my low journey through the scary wooded dark basin.

Just keep looking forward to the bright sunshine that I will be facing.

I realize with every hill top conquest there is the other side of that peak.

Searching for answers you seek for my soul to keep.

Listening to words you pretend not to hear.

You always speak in lingoes that cause fear.

Declaration of your thoughts will release your inner tears.

Losing people while on my route will be the hardest to capture.

After losing a person that was sharing a quest on my path, I will never stop my adventure.

Knowing that the ones that go before me I will never lose, they are always with me.

I am at ease with the thought that they would want me to walk my path to see all I can see.

We will see each other once again at the top of the highest elevation.

I want to be able to tell them I missed them every second, but I had strength to carry on with jubilation.

THOUGHTS AND DREAMS

If there was a way to see my thoughts and dreams.

Most people would run and scream.

I think if we could see other thoughts and dreams.

We would be shocked at what we see to the extreme.

It is better to let people keep their own thoughts and dreams.

So, we can be amazed of what we can see to remain as a team.

That is why they are called your thoughts and dreams.

We only share with people that will not bring down our esteem.

Keep having your thoughts and dreams.

TREE

Everybody's family tree looks similar.

There are branches that are high.

Stretching to the sky.

Wanting to fly.

Then there are low hangers.

They are bottom feeders.

Far from the leaders.

The branches that fill the tree.

They are the strength of the monarch.

Always looking after the bark.

The muscle of every family tree.

What holds the tree together.

Are the elder roots.

With the passing of an elder root.

One of the branches must become a root.

The tree will fall without strong roots.

TRUE

Many days I fight with thoughts in my mind.

The doubts always consume the day.

Never knowing what it is I will find.

Or what the voices in my head will say.

The hardest days are when I lose me.

Lost in the cavern of my mind.

Searching every corner to be free.

Trying not to be left behind.

Seems I'm always crying inside.

Embarrassed of the person I have become.

Feeling like my insides has died.

Just wanting to feel numb.

Needing the one who carried the cross of my shame.

Two Voices

My fear is that my words make you stop singing.

I need your help to sing with all my being.

How do you replace a voice that will not sing with you?

This empty room makes me blue.

All your silence came with hostility.

Is the silence worth the animosity?

When your voice is gone and leaves your nothingness.

You will have no use for bitterness?

The time that we wasted mad and not singing in harmony.

It is hard for me trying to be someone else with conformity.

I regret the times we can't LOVE instead of hate.

I take all the blame for my fate.

I always find a way to sing off key.

I hope it will not keep you away from me.

You make my voice sing at a different pitch.

We have always found our niche.

My world needs to hear our melody.

VOICES

Always in good company, being the only person in the room.

All the voices in my head speaking at once makes my mind set off a boom.

I am having a great conversation with no one else talking.

My secrets are always known by each person in my head pestering.

Is it better to feel pain than feel nothing at all in your soul?

I never trust what my mind is telling me because they want to take control.

Feeling bruised and battered from the verbal attacks in my mind.

Fighting with the abusive voices daily is always a grind.

How come I can't silent the noise like others claim they can?

I wished I was as strong as Adam West while he was Batman.

Pow Bam I would kick butt with the entire negative thought in my head.

Then I could be normal like everyone else say's they are and not be misread.

But in real life I think it is normal to have things going on that makes everyone feel just like ME.

WHEELS OF LIFE

The wheels of life spin slowly when we are in our youth.

The light shines bright on our days of truth.

The innocents and care free days can seem never ending.

One day we wake and become young adults with time that is surrendering.

The world is at your fingertips, not knowing what to grab hold of or leave behind.

Friends and Family that we thought were close seem to fade and decline.

The wheels of life spin much faster as we age, with no brakes to slow it down.

With any luck we understand what really matters with the short time before we drown.

The true family and friends that you thought were gone will always have your back.

Thinking back on the time your mind was sharp as a tack.

Learning that what truly matters is not only how much you have loved, but how much you are loved.

WHY

Why is it one day I wake and the demons in my head are silent.

I feel normal and all at once it feels I have been hit with a mallet.

The demons tell me that I am alone and my body has that empty feeling.

If I had any self-esteem it is ripped from my whole being.

I hide it the darkest corner of my head.

My only thought is to run to my safe place back in bed.

They remind me constantly that my worth is immaterial.

I want to be happy but it is hard when it feels like everything is surreal.

The demons drain my spirit and energy so all that is left is a shell.

It can feel like all the blood has been taken out of my body and I turn pale.

I cherish the few moments that I feel like a partial normal person.

More times I feel it is me against the world and I feel like cursing.

The demons tell me that the world would be better without me.

All I can think of is when the next bad thing will make me flee.

Peacefulness!!!!!!

WORDS

The dumb words that come from my brain.

How do I know if the words I put together even make sense.

I'm not sure where they come from, they just cause strain.

Having people read my words can make me tense.

Not knowing where the words come from seems foolish.

Maybe they come from deep thoughts.

Maybe I think it makes me coolish.

Maybe it brings out faults.

Wherever they come from I hope someone relates.

If only with one word or sentence.

You

Angry at the stars.

Because you feel you will never go far.

Wishing you had wings.

So, you could fly and sing.

But you are listening to the voices in your head.

Always a Doubting Thomas of impending dread.

You're too scared to take a leap of trust.

Not knowing you have been sprinkled with angel dust.

Being angry with things that are not set on your path.

Have trust in your visions, attack the world fierce on your path.

Fly high with no regrets or fears.

Know that you are doing what you are meant to do through the years.

If today is your last, go with a loud voice being you.

DARRELL SOMERS

Darrell Somers is an Artist and Author from Mesquite, Texas. He spent many years ignoring thoughts to start painting and writing.

After painting his first painting in 2011 and writing his first poem in 2017, they became his passion. His paintings are whimsical and his writings are inspirational with a side of whimsy.

His artwork can be seen at Bear Cave Coffee, Flying Squirrel Coffee, Dirty Job Brewery, Savor Coffee, and Pour Wine Bar, and several other places in North Texas.

He graduated from Mesquite High School and achieved his bachelor's degree from Western Governor's University.

You can follow Darrell on Instagram at somers_art

Be sure to check out Darrell's other book "My Walk" where he shares his thoughts about walking a faith journey.

All his books are available at Amazon, Ingram and other online and retail outlets.

www.ingramcontent.com/pod-product-compliance
Lightning Source LLC
Chambersburg PA
CBHW051542120626
46551CB00013B/1333